FOOTBALL'S RUDEST QUOTES

Insults, Swearing, and Plenty of Balls

Harry Jones

Publisher Information

Published by Harry Jones

Copyright © 2020 Harry Jones

Contents

Let's start with some swearing

❝ I'm not a wheeler dealer, f*ck off. I'm not a f*cking wheeler and dealer, don't even, don't say that, I'm a f*cking football manager. **❞**

Harry Redknapp

Harry Redknapp doesn't just do transfers

❝ Neymar is the Justin Bieber of football. Brilliant on the old YouTube. Cat p*ss in reality... **❞**

Joey Barton

❝ He actually looks a little twat, that Totti. **❞**

— Ron Atkinson

❝ It was a crap start to a game. There you have it, can you print all that? F**king rubbish, absolute tosh. Drivel. Sh*te. Bullsh*t. That's what I thought of it. Did that help? I'm quite pleased, apart from the fact that's given them the poxy result, I'm f**king livid about it – of course I am. So, there you have it. **❞**

— Mick McCarthy

Mick McCarthy wasn't impressed with his team

" Who do you think you are having meetings about me? You were a crap player and you are a crap manager. The only reason I have any dealings with you is that somehow you are the manager of my country and you're not even Irish, you English c*nt! **"**

— **Roy Keane**

Roy Keane has a little chat with Republic of Ireland manager Mick McCarthy

" When I saw Owen score that goal for England against Argentina in 1998 I thought, 'You little sh*t!' Even aged 10, I knew they couldn't allow him that much space. **"**

— **Sergio Aguero**

Sergio Aguero on Michael Owen

❛❛ I told him in no uncertain terms to go and f*ck himself. **❜❜**

— Charlie George

Don Revie subs Charlie when he was playing for England.
Charlie suggests it was the wrong decision

❛❛ I must say that I have seen quite a few Spurs players kiss the badge and then f*ck off. I am still here. **❜❜**

— Benoit Assou-Ekotto

Football is just a job for Benoit

❝ Go tell him to quit f**king around. Alfredo Di Stéfano, Cruyff, Messi are the greatest that I saw. **❞**

— **Maradona**

Maradona is not a fan of Ronaldo

❝ I'd waited long enough. I f*cking hit him hard. The ball was there (I think). Take that you c*nt. And don't ever stand over me sneering about fake injuries. **❞**

— **Roy Keane**

Roy Keane on tackling Alf Inge Haaland

❝ You're a big-nosed French tw*t. ❞

— **Paul Merson**

Paul Merson to David Ginola during a cup match. Ginola
scored shortly after

**❝ Him and his fat mate should be sh*tting it
if I decide to write a book. There'll be no
holding back on those two muppets. ❞**

— **Joey Barton**

Joey Barton blasts his old bosses at Newcastle

❝ You're a f*cking bottler Incey! You cannae handle the stage, can you? You are a f*cking bottler! **❞**

— **Alex Ferguson**

Alex Ferguson – a big fan of Paul Ince

❝ Shut yours you f*cking old c*nt. **❞**

— **Alan Pardew**

Alan Pardew to Man City manager Manuel Pellegrini

❝ Most footballers are knobs. **❞**

— Joey Barton

❝ Mancini said, 'You're an idiot and I don't know why I bought you'. I hate people who say 'Mario, you played well', then say to others, 'Mario was sh*t'. Roberto has never lied to me. **❞**

— Mario Balotelli

Did they really say that?!?

❝ Joe Cole has got his socks down and really looks the business... actually Mourinho's pulled him off now... **❞**

— Alan Smith

❝ Julian Dicks is everywhere. It's like they've got 11 Dicks on the field. **❞**

Radio Commentary

❝ He's been feeling his groin for a week now. **❞**

— **Alan Shearer**

Alan Shearer explaining an Obafemi Martins injury

❝ Martin Keown is up everybody's backsides. **❞**

— **Trevor Brooking**

❝ I personally will always have a soft spot for Willie. **❞**

— **Kevin Keegan**

That's Willie Donachie apparently

" He'll take some pleasure from that, Brian Carey. He and Steve Bull have been having it off all afternoon. **"**

— Ron Atkinson

" Sometimes it is good to score at 43 seconds... and sometimes it is good to last a little longer. **"**

— Roberto Di Matteo

" Sometimes you want Obertan to open his legs and do something a bit exciting... **"**

— Alan Pardew

" He signals to the bench with his groin. **"**

— Mark Bright

❝ Thank you all for participating in the CR7 Boys Underwear Competition it's been a real pleasure to see all of your photos. ❞
—Cristiano Ronaldo

That moment when you read back your tweet and realise some people might take it the wrong way

❝ Once Tony Daley opens his legs, you've got a problem. ❞

— Howard Wilkinson

PSV have got a lot of pace up front. They're capable of exposing themselves.

— Barry Venison

I've had to come out of the dressing room because I don't want to get too excited.

— Bobby Robson

Insults

"" He's a flatterer. And his final ball is pathetic. Pathetic. He fools the public but he doesn't fool me. **""**

— **Bobby Robson**

Bobby Robson on Steve McManaman

"" Arsene Wenger has put me down a few times. The annoying thing is, he does it intelligently and I hate that. Sometimes I want to punch him on the nose. **""**

— **Tony Adams**

❝ How the f*cking hell did he miss that? My missus could have scored that... You keep pussyfooting around with people – what am I supposed to say? Really good try? Really unlucky? He's really done his best with that? **❞**

— **Harry Redknapp**

Darren Bent misses an easy chance – Harry is unimpressed

❝ He drove me mad in training. Technically, he was outstanding but he always seemed to be playing with his hair. **❞**

— **Harry Redknapp**

Harry Redknapp on Gareth Bale

❝ I would rather sit down and have a cuppa with Neil Ruddock, who broke my leg in two places in 1996, than with Teddy Sheringham, who I've pretty much detested for the past 15 years. **❞**

— Andy Cole

❝ He's a bully, a f*cking big-time Charlie. **❞**

— Alex Ferguson

Alex Ferguson on Paul Ince

❝ He just needs to make his brain work. That is his only problem. **❞**

— **Roberto Mancini**

Roberto Mancini on Mario Balotelli

❝ He is one of those players – and I don't think he will be unhappy with me saying it – that some days you look at him in training and he is useless. **❞**

— **Joe Hart**

Joe Hart on Sergio Aguero

“ Laurent Robert said I was picking the wrong team – at the time I was, because he was in it. **”**

— Bobby Robson

“ Away from home our fans are fantastic, I'd call them the hardcore fans. But at home they have a few drinks and probably the prawn sandwiches, and they don't realise what's going on out on the pitch. I don't think some of the people who come to Old Trafford can spell 'football', never mind understand it. **”**

— Roy Keane

The Ref is always right

❛❛ I'm a bit proud of my first red card as coach. I approached the fourth official and said: 'How many mistakes are allowed here? If it is 15, you have one more.' **❜❜**

— Jürgen Klopp

❛❛ The referee, he ate too much for Christmas. He was not in good form. **❜❜**

— Roberto Mancini

Roberto Mancini not happy with Kevin Friend

❝ I personally think referees should be wired up to a couple of electrodes and they should be allowed to make three mistakes before you run 50,000 volts through their genitals. **❞**

— John Gregory

❝ The referee made a difference. All credit to him, he scored a good second goal for them. I was happy for him. He deserves a good mention. **❞**

— Arsene Wenger

Arsene Wenger politely disputes a penalty decision

❝ I never comment on referees and I'm not going to break the habit of a lifetime for that prat. **❞**

— Ron Atkinson

❝ The referee made three mistakes only. The red card, playing too much time at the end of the first half and the penalty. Apart from that he was good. **❞**

— Avram Grant

❝ If he fouls you he normally picks you up, but the referee doesn't see what he picks you up by. **❞**

— **Ryan Giggs**

Ryan Giggs on Dennis Wise

❝ Clubs come away from Anfield choking on their own vomit and biting their own tongues knowing they have been done by the referee. **❞**

— **Alex Ferguson**

Alex Ferguson – Liverpool's biggest fan

Football is such a polite sport

❝ Carlton covers every blade of grass on the pitch – but then you have to if your first touch is that crap. **❞**

— Dave Jones

Dave Jones, motivating Carlton Palmer at Southampton

❝ I was with David the fateful night he first saw the Spice Girls on telly and said, 'See that girl who can't dance or sing? I'm going to marry her'. **❞**

— Gary Neville

Gary Neville on how David Beckham fell for Victoria

“ Viv Anderson has p*ssed a fatness test. **”**
— John Helm

We think he passed a fitness test, but aren't totally sure

“ If you were a racehorse, they'd shoot you. **”**
— Francis Lee

Francis Lee thinks teammate Mike Summerbee is past it

“ The fans who gave me stick are the ones who still point at aeroplanes. **”**
— Ian Wright

❝ There will have to be a bubonic plague for me to pick Di Canio. **❞**

— **Giovanni Trapattoni**

So, that's a no then?

❝ What John Carew does with a football, I can do with an orange. **❞**

— **Zlatan Ibrahimovic**

Zlatan being Zlatan

“ My scout told me this lad had football in his blood. I said, 'Aye, but it hasn't reached his legs yet'. **”**

— Bill Shankly

“ Alan Shearer is boring – we call him Mary Poppins. He never gets into trouble. **”**

— Freddy Shepherd

A little
bit of news

" I don't give any of you credibility. You talk about wanting to have an association with people here and you wonder why I don't get on with you? But you're a f*cking embarrassment. One of these days the door is going to be shut on you permanently. "

— **Alex Ferguson**

Alex Ferguson – a big fan of the media

❝ I've always said there's a place for the press, but they haven't dug it yet. **❞**
—— **Tommy Docherty**

Alex Ferguson wasn't the first Man United manager to have a "difficult" relationship with the media

❝ I'm off to my 300-acre farm. You lot can bugger off to your council houses. **❞**
—— **Ken Bates**

Ken Bates to the press after the Blues were relegated

In the bedroom

❝ Andy Gray is an ugly b*stard in the morning and I can vouch for that because I've slept with him a few times. **❞**

— John Bailey

❝ I sorted out the team formation last night lying in bed with the wife. When your husband's as ugly as me, you'd only want to talk football in bed. **❞**

— Harry Redknapp

❝ I haven't a clue how many women I had – four or five maybe. But I regret it deeply. **❞**

— **Kieron Dyer**

Kieron Dyer "regrets" what he did on holiday in Aya Napa

❝ He constantly wants sex because he thinks he can wear his groin out if it's being fixed. It's exhausting. **❞**

— **Harry Kewell**

Harry Kewell had a groin operation planned. His wife is a little concerned that he thinks he's getting a replacement and can use this one up!

" I usually don't have sex. Not on the same day. I say no thanks. I guess that, mentally, I want to keep the feeling in my feet and that's why. I think the feeling sort of disappears out of your feet if you have sex before. I have tried before and my feet felt like concrete when you are supposed to kick the ball. **"**

— Freddie Ljungberg

" It was as if I'd spent ages making love to the most beautiful woman in the world only to be kicked out of bed five minutes before the climax. **"**

— Peter Storey

Worried about not being picked for the FA Cup final

❝ I love tackling. It's better than sex. A great tackle gets everybody pumped up. **❞**

— Paul Ince

❝ I would not sign for another club, not even for 15 million dollars. However, it would be different if they were to instead offer me 15 different women from all around the world. I would tell the club chairman: 'Please let me make these women happy – I will satisfy them like they have never been satisfied before.' **❞**

— Sasa Curcic

" One of the first things Arsene Wenger did at Arsenal was to make sure players couldn't get pay-per-view in hotels. If players are exciting themselves quite a few times then it's going to affect their physical condition. **"**

— Tony Adams

" After you've scored a goal it's just orgasmic ... if you asked me just after a game I'd says its better than sex, but if you asked me just after sex I'd say, 'Forget it, mate.' **"**

— Trevor Sinclair

❝ I didn't get too many women running after me. It was their f*cking husbands who'd be after me. **❞**

— Charlie George

❝ Our central defenders, Doherty and Anthony Gardner, were fantastic and I told them that when they go to bed tonight they should think of each other. **❞**

— David Pleat

❝ At first he told us to wear boxing gloves in bed on Friday nights, then later he would tell us to send the wife to her mother. **❞**

— Ian St John

Bill Shankly has one method...

❝ For him, his players' sexual activity must take place before midnight in order to get a good night's sleep – even if they are free tomorrow. He said that he placed this rule on Messi and his muscles improved since. **❞**

— Samir Nasri

...and Pep Guardiola has another

" Gazza said that scoring was better than an orgasm. Lee Chapman reckoned it wasn't as good. I'll go with Pele – he thought it was about the same. **"**

— Ryan Giggs

" We play every three days. How can I be a good husband if I don't make love before each game? **"**

— Frank Leboeuf

❝ I was asked which one I'd choose, Viana or Viagra? That's easy. Saturday afternoon, Viana. Saturday night, Viagra. **❞**

— **Bobby Robson**

Bobby was famous for getting names mixed up. Hopefully he didn't this time

❝ It's the equivalent to being with the prettiest woman in the world and only sleeping with her once a month. I prefer to sleep with someone slightly less pretty every night! **❞**

— **Gérard Houllier**

Gérard Houllier didn't want a return to international management

A friendly rivalry

@#%!

❝ My greatest challenge is not what's happening at the moment, my greatest challenge was knocking Liverpool right off their f*cking perch. And you can print that. **❞**

— Alex Ferguson

❝ When I called Coventry supporters a bunch of w*nkers, it was the best 15 grand I ever spent. **❞**

— Ian Wright

Ian Wright paying his fine with a smile

❝ I think Sheffield Wednesday are a very poor football team. They are like a man who's got diarrhea who can't get his trousers down. **❞**

— Rodney Marsh

❝ My team mates advised me to visit the city first. I went to have a look at Middlesborough and decided I was better off in Parma. **❞**

— Antonio Rattin

❝ I always dreamed of winning the league at White Hart Lane. So I left and joined Arsenal. **❞**

— Sol Campbell

Sol Campbell endearing himself to the Spurs fans.

❝ I'd rather go and collect stamps than stick on that shirt. **❞**

— Steven Taylor

Steven Taylor, when asked if he'd play for Sunderland

❝ I'm often asked how this Rangers team compares with the Lisbon Lions. I have to be honest and say I think it would be a draw but, then, some of us are getting on for 60. **❞**

— **Bertie Auld**

Bertie won the 1967 European Cup with Celtic. Still not a fan of Rangers when asked about them 25 years later.

❝ If Chelsea are naive and pure then I'm Little Red Riding Hood. **❞**

— **Rafa Benitez**

Rafa Benitez doesn't believe Jose Mourinho

" More football later, but first let's see the goals from the Scottish Cup final. **"**

— Des Lynam

" This is an unusual Scotland side because they have good players. **"**

— Javier Clemente

" I have watched Barnsley and it is clear they are not Real Madrid. **"**

— Roberto Mancini

More
lovely quotes

((It's an incredible rise to stardom; at 17 you're more likely to get a call from Michael Jackson than Sven-Göran Eriksson. **))**

— Gordon Strachan

Gordon Strachan really went there, when Wayne Rooney got an England call up

((Can you imagine how the players would react if I turned up one day and said, 'I'd like you to meet Cock and Dick'? **))**

— Martin Jol

Martin Jol's brothers are called Cock and Dick. He doesn't think they should try and get jobs in England. We agree

❝ When I ran towards The Kop I could almost hear them saying, 'Who's this skinny little tw*t?' ❞

— **Steven Gerrard**

Steven Gerrard on his Anfield debut

❝ People are comparing him to Brian Clough, but Cloughy had the sexual attraction of a plate. ❞

Hunter Davies

Hunter Davies on Jose Mourinho

❝ For the first time we have two central defenders who have been pillars and not pillocks. **❞**

— **Bobby Robson**

Bobby Robson on Darren Peacock & Steve Howey

❝ I told Balotelli that if he played with me 10 years ago, I would have maybe punched him in the head on a daily basis. I don't speak with him every day, otherwise I would need a psychologist. **❞**

— **Roberto Mancini**

❝ He only has to fart during a warm-up and they're singing his name from the rafters. **❞**

— Ashley Cole

Ashley Cole on Freddie Ljungberg

❝ They couldn't really call me 'Spunky' when the younger fans are around. So they settled on 'H'. It's Cockney rhyming slang: Harry Monk – spunk. **❞**

— David Seaman

** I worked hard all my life for this. Those who say I don't deserve anything, that it all came easy, can kiss my ar*e. **

— Diego Maradona

** I read this piece by the car man, Jeremy Clarkson, saying a footballer goes out in the morning, gets in his Aston Martin, forgets to take a drugs test, takes coke, has a drink, then shags a bird. And that was 'a day in the life of a footballer'. But a lot of players are decent fellas. **

— Frank Lampard

Carry on footballing

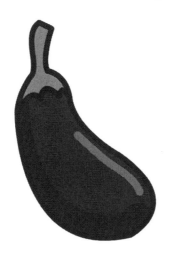

❝ He's pulling him off! The Spanish manager is pulling his captain off. **❞**

—George Hamilton

❝ I was saying the other day, how often the most vulnerable area for goalies is between their legs. **❞**

— Andy Gray

" There's lots of balls dropping off people. **"**

— Ron Atkinson

" Their forward got a lucky squeeze from the defender. **"**

— Ron Atkinson

" For such a small man Maradona gets great elevation on his balls. **"**

— David Pleat

❝ Ardiles strokes the ball like it was a part of his anatomy. **❞**

— Jimmy Magee

❝ Jean Tigana has spent the entire first half inside Liam Brady's shorts. **❞**

— Jimmy Magee

❝ Fabregas literally carries ten yards of space around in his shorts. **❞**

— Ray Wilkins

❝ Fulham are growing in confidence now and will believe that they can impregnate this Spurs defence. **❞**

— Robbie Earle

❝ There's no doubt Bentley has balls – and plenty of 'em. **❞**

— Harry Redknapp

Harry Redknapp on David Bentley

ll Bottle is a quality too, you know. It's not just about ball control and being clever. Sometimes you have to show the world what's between your legs. **ll**

— Graeme Souness

ll Brazil – they're so good it's like they are running around the pitch playing with themselves. **ll**

— John Motson

❝ Let's hope it's not a case of sore grapes. **❞**

— Alan Brazil

❝ Players win games, but managers give you the impotence to go and do it. **❞**

— Lee Fowler

❝ That's often the best place to beat a goalkeeper, isn't it, between the legs? **❞**

— Clive Tyldesley

❝ The goal that Charlton scored has aroused Arsenal. **❞**

— George Graham

❝ Tore's got a groin strain and he's been playing with it. **❞**

— Alex McLeish

Alex McLeish on Tore André Flo

❝ Where his balls go, you will be quite surprised. **❞**

— Arsene Wenger

Arsene Wenger on Denilson

Welcome to England

❝ Monday, Tuesday, W*nkday, Thursday, Friday, Saturday and Sunday. ❞

— **Paul Gascoigne**

Gazza helps Mirandinha learn the days of the week

❝ First thing we taught him was: 'Tottenham are sh*t'. ❞

— **Ian Wright**

Ian Wright helps Patrick Vieira with his English

❝ At a French club they buy you champagne and cake on your birthday. Here they shove your face in the mud. **❞**

— Frank Leboeuf

❝ Dennis Bergkamp told me the Dutch always thought of the English as strong but stupid. **❞**

— Tony Adams

" Places like this are the soul of English football. The crowd is magnificent, saying 'f*** off Mourinho' and so on. **"**

— Jose Mourinho

Jose on a visit to Bramall Lane

" I have not got accustomed to English life. The food is truly disastrous and it rains all the time. **"**

— Patrice Evra

❝ Yes, I swear a lot. But the advantage is that having played abroad I can choose a different language from the referee's. **❞**
— Jurgen Klinsmann

❝ I just told [the translator] to tell him to f*cking run around a bit. The boy himself just kept nodding his head. He might be thinking inside, 'What's this t*sser saying to me?' **❞**
— Harry Redknapp

Harry Redknapp on managing Roman Pavlyuchenko

Sweet talk

" I spent a lot of money on booze, birds, and fast cars. The rest I just squandered. "

— George Best

" Once in Norway I went up to him, put my arm around him and asked him how he was, just so I could put a lemon on his shoulder without him noticing. It was a silly joke and gave the lads a good laugh, but George was not happy about it. He was even less happy when Niall Quinn once put a condom there. "

— Tony Adams

Tony Adams on George Graham

❝ People always say I shouldn't be burning the candle at both ends. Maybe they haven't got a big enough candle. **❞**

— George Best

❝ I couldn't be more chuffed if I were a badger at the start of the mating season. **❞**

— Ian Holloway

❝ You see him, the face of an angel but he is a son of a b***h ... One day I was eating, I left my phone on the table, and he sent a text offering Galliani [the AC Milan vice-president] my sister. **❞**

— **Gennaro Gattuso**

Gennaro Gattuso on Andrea Pirlo

❝ Don't you dare put it on quick spin or I'll f*cking brae the lot of you. **❞**

— **Paul Gascoigne**

Gazza takes precautions before getting inside the dry cleaner at the training ground

As for that rumour about me having an erection while I was lying there, that's b*llocks. I never got an erection after scoring a goal.

— Charlie George

Charlie George scotches rumours about his
1971 FA Cup Final winner

'Wait until you come to Turkey' was the shout, with fingers being passed across throats. And that was just the kitman!

— Gareth Southgate

Gareth Southgate enjoying Turkish hospitality

❝ There was plenty of fellers who would kick your b*llocks off. **❞**

— Nat Lofthouse

❝ He's grinning. 'You pr*ck'. He gestures dismissively. The red card comes out. Shearer's right. I am a pr*ck. **❞**

— Roy Keane

Roy Keane after a little rough and tumble with Alan Shearer

“ In the last ten minutes I was breathing out of my ar*e. **”**

— Clinton Morrison

“ Dogs are very honest. They'll never let you down. They'll play football with you in the garden ... and at the end they'll crap all over your lawn. **”**

— Mark Viduka

" Could you get us all a pair of those Calvin Klein's? We want the special ones like yours, the ones with a sock down the front. We've seen you in the shower and you're really not that big. **"**

— **Dennis Bergkamp**

Dennis Bergkamp on Freddie Ljungberg

" Footballers are only interested in drinking, clothes and the size of their willies. **"**

— **Karren Brady**

** Dennis Wise grabbed my tit. I had five finger marks around the nipple, like a love bite. That took some explaining to the missus. **

— Jason McAteer

** Fiorentina start the second half attacking their fans; just the way they like things. **

— Ray Wilkins

" Dennis Bergkamp is such a nice man, such a tremendous gentleman, with such a lovely family. It's going to be hard for me to kick him. **"**

— Tony Adams

Before playing against Dennis in an England v Holland game

" From time to time, I'm a jerk. **"**

— Samir Nasri

❝ I got some girl's knickers through the post the other day but I didn't like them. To be honest, they didn't fit. **❞**

— Jamie Redknapp

@#%!

❝ I kicked a few full-backs in my time but I always sent them flowers afterwards. **❞**

— Mike Summerbee

❝ I knew he had a stomach problem because I was in the toilet after him. ❞

— Kenny Dalglish

Kenny gives too much info about subbing Daniel Agger

❝ I may have looked calm but my backside was going some. ❞

— Alan Shearer

Alan Shearer, after scoring a penalty in an FA Cup semi-final

❛❛ I never thought it would take so long for me to have a chance to put it on. It does smell. I have only cleaned it once or twice. **❜❜**

— Jonas Gutierrez

Jonas famously pulled a mask out of his pants when he scored his first goal for Newcastle. Maybe not a good idea for someone who very rarely scores!

❛❛ That's the way I am and I always will be. After all, I kick Laurent Robert in training – and he's one of our players. **❜❜**

— Andy Griffin

" There's no problem with Jermain. I wouldn't swap him for Miss World — he would probably swap me for Miss World though. "

— Martin Jol

Martin Jol after talk of a bust-up with Jermain Defoe

" Even when they had Moore, Hurst and Peters, West Ham's average finish was about 17th, which just shows how cr*p the other eight of us were. "

— Harry Redknapp

❝ Have you seen my a*se? It's like an Alsatian's. **❞**

— Steven Gerrard

❝ At White Hart Lane, the two teams were going down the tunnel and I felt this tugging from behind. As I was about to step on to the pitch with 30,000 people watching, Gazza was trying to pull my shorts down. Luckily, they were tied firmly or I would have made my entrance with my kecks around my ankles. **❞**

— David Seaman

" I was welcomed to Ibrox by McCoist and Durrant spraying Ralgex all over my underpants. "

— Iain Ferguson

" I'll get in trouble with my girlfriend if I play – I don't think she'll be too happy if I'm chasing Totti all over Rome. "

— Jonathan Woodgate

Jonathan Woodgate kicking off his career as a comedian

❝ If you'd given me the choice of going out and beating four men and smashing a goal in from 30 yards against Liverpool or going to bed with Miss World, it would have been a difficult choice. Luckily, I had both. **❞**

— George Best

❝ In 1969 I gave up women and alcohol. It was the worst 20 minutes of my life. **❞**

— George Best

" The gaffer said at the end of his team talk, 'Has anybody got any questions?' 'Yes', I said. 'Where do babies come from?' "

— Brian McClair

Brian McClair risks the wrath of Alex Ferguson

" To be marooned on a desert island with an endless supply of lager, women and Sky TV. "

— Ian Walker

Ian Walker's dreams for the future

" Being chairman of Tottenham was like having diarrhoea. "

— Alan Sugar

" Well, I won't be picking it for a while! "

— Andy Linighan

Andy Linighan after breaking his nose

" After six weeks in the England camp, even Jack Charlton could look attractive. "

— George Cohen

Printed in Great Britain
by Amazon

49979256R00066